Praise for *One Blackbird at a Time*

Although these poems begin in the classroom, their reach feels limitless and wild. Here, seemingly anecdotal encounters with the work of Henry James, Virginia Woolf, or Robert Frost spiral into meditations on the lives of others, the complexities of our ethical decisions, the nuances of human relationships, and the certainties of mortality. It would be easy to say this is a book about teaching—it is!—but it's also a book about how our experience of reading humanizes us and shapes our experience of the world and other people. Wendy Barker's poems are rich, complex, and shimmering with energy and intelligence.

—Kevin Prufer, author of *In a Beautiful Country* and *Churches*

Wendy Barker's *One Blackbird at a Time* is a humorous and poignant meditation on what it is to be a professor of literature, what it could possibly mean in our era of visual literacy. *One Blackbird at a Time* makes a case for poetry—the poetry of the canon and the poetry of the now, i.e. Barker's own poetry. She takes on the big questions with smarts and a disarming joie de vivre. Her work is the best argument against "those who can't ___, teach." This is one can-do volume! Anyone who's ever been a student will want to read *One Blackbird at a Time* to find out what it is like on the other side of the desk.

—Denise Duhamel, author of *Blowout* and *Ka-Ching!*

Like a favorite class, the whole of *One Blackbird at a Time* is greater than the sum of its parts, although the individual poems stand up exquisitely well on their own. Decades of teachers and students will see themselves in these poems.

—David Dooley, *Paterson Literary Review*

The poems begin depicting classroom discussions of literature—largely the standards of introductory surveys—then deftly pivot to smart, ranging meditations on contemporary culture, family connection, and loss . . . . And one needn't be an educator to delight in Barker's generous humanist vision.

—Benjamin S. Grossberg, *Antioch Review*

Wendy Barker's keen eye for detail results in one of the most exciting and original poetry collections I have read for a long time.

—Valerie Morton, *Galatea Resurrects*

One *Blackbird* at a Time

Other Books by Wendy Barker

POETRY

Books

Nothing Between Us: The Berkeley Years
Poems from Paradise
Way of Whiteness
Let the Ice Speak
Winter Chickens and Other Poems

Chapbooks

Things of the Weather
Between Frames
Eve Remembers

Translations

Tagore: Final Poems (with Saranindranath Tagore)

PROSE

Poems' Progress
The House Is Made of Poetry: The Art of Ruth Stone, co-edited with Sandra M. Gilbert
Lunacy of Light: Emily Dickinson and the Experience of Metaphor

One *Blackbird* at a Time

Wendy Barker

Winner of the John Ciardi Prize for Poetry
Selected by Alice Friman

BkMk Press
University of Missouri-Kansas City

BkMk Press
University of Missouri-Kansas City
5101 Rockhill Road
Kansas City, MO 64110
www.umkc.edu/bkmk

Financial assistance for this project has been provided by
the Missouri Arts Council, a state agency.

Executive Editor: Robert Stewart
Managing Editor: Ben Furnish
Associate Editor: Michelle Boisseau
Assistant Managing Editor: Cynthia Beard
Cover art: Michael Mayhugh

BkMk Press wishes to thank Marie Mayhugh, Cameron Morse,
Anders Carlson, Brittany Green.

The John Ciardi Prize for Poetry thanks Walter Bargen, Greg Field, Lindsey Martin-Bowen,
Linda Rodriguez, Maryfrances Wagner.

Library of Congress Cataloging-in-Publication Data

Barker, Wendy.
  [Poems. Selections]
  One blackbird at a time / Wendy Barker.
      pages ; cm
  "Winner of the John Ciardi Prize for Poetry selected by Alice Friman."
  ISBN 978-1-943491-03-2 (acid-free paper)
  I. Title.
  PS3552.A67124A6 2015
  811'.54--dc23
                            2015036459

ISBN 978-1-943491-03-2

This book is set in Garamond and Gill Sans.

Acknowledgments

I am grateful to the editors of the following magazines, in which some of these poems first appeared, at times in slightly different versions.

Barn Owl Review	"Whenever We've Dipped into *Walden*"
Cerise Press	"In the Seminar, Trying to Launch *Passage to India*" and "Waking Over *Call It Sleep*"
Connecticut Review	"Arriving at Wallace Stevens in the 13th Week" and "Emily in the Classroom"
Crab Creek Review	"After Spring Break, Arriving at Pound's 'In a Station of the Metro,'" "Alone in the Museum's Greek Collection," and "Coming to Cather"
Diode	"Langston Hughes' 'Weary Blues'" and "His Eyelashes Are Not Tarantulas"
Gettysburg Review	"On Teaching Too Many Victorian Novels in Too Short a Space of Time During Which I Become"
Lips	"I'd Said It Would Be"
Matter Press	"Wang Wei in the Workshop"
Mid-American Review	"Why I Dread Teaching *The Sun Also Rises*" and "In Our Class on Roethke"
New Letters	"I'm Not Sure the Cherry Is the 'Loveliest of Trees'"
Paterson Literary Review	"About That 'One Art,'" "Innisfree, They Get," and "Next-to-Last Week in the Senior Workshop"
Southern Review	"I Hate Telling People I Teach English," "Teaching 'The Red Wheelbarrow' the 30th Time," "Teaching *Mrs. Dalloway* I'm Thinking," "The Last Time I Taught Robert Frost," "Truth, Beauty, and the Intro Poetry Workshop," "Books, Bath Towels, and Beyond," "Rereading *The Golden Bowl*," "Ending the Semester in American Lit," and "The Morning After Our Second Ecopoetry Class"
Water-Stone Review	"Preparing Jeffers 'Vulture' Before Class"

"Books, Bath Towels, and Beyond" is included in *The Best American Poetry 2013*, eds. Denise Duhamel and David Lehman (Scribner). "Teaching *Mrs. Dalloway* I'm Thinking" and "Teaching 'The Red Wheelbarrow' the 30th Time" were reprinted on VerseDaily, www.versedaily.org. "Teaching 'The Red Wheelbarrow' the 30th Time," "Innisfree, They Get," "Langston Hughes' 'Weary Blues,'" and "In Our Class on Roethke" are all included in *Poets on Growth*, eds. Peter LaBerge and Talin Tahajian (Math Paper). "Why I Dread Teaching *The Sun Also Rises*" was reprinted in *Women Write Resistance: Poets Resist Gender Violence*, ed. Laura Madeline Wiseman (Hyacinth Girl). "Ending the Semester in American Lit" is included in *Raising Lilly Ledbetter: Women Poets Occupy the Workspace*, eds. Carolyne Wright, M. L. Lyons, and Eugenia Toledo (Lost Horse Press).

I owe reams of thanks to the generous friends who provided help with a number of these poems: Kacee Belcher, Ralph Black, Chana Bloch, David Dooley, Sandra M. Gilbert, Jeannine Keenan, Alicia Ostriker, and David Ray Vance. Denise Duhamel, Catherine Kasper, and Barbara Ras made excellent suggestions for the manuscript. And I owe much to the University of Texas at San Antonio for institutional support, especially Bernadette Andrea, Mark Bayer, Bridget Drinka, and Daniel J. Gelo. I'm extremely grateful to Alice Friman, and to Michelle Boisseau and Ben Furnish of BkMk Press for such excellent care and advice. And without Jacqueline Kolosov and my two Bolinas Salon compadres, Kevin Clark and Hannah Stein, who spent more time with these poems than they should have, this entire collection could never have taken shape. I must also offer heartfelt thanks to my son, David Barker, and my sisters, Trisha McConnell and Liza Piatt, for their understanding, support, and encouragement. And finally, I want to express immeasurable gratitude to my husband Steven G. Kellman, who read and reread drafts upon drafts of these poems and whose quiet, dependable rhythms make dailiness a poem.

Contents

Foreword

Wendy Barker's *One Blackbird at a Time* is not a how-to book, an instruction manual about teaching literature in today's college classroom, although there's many a valuable tip one can learn here. Nor is the book a sort of memoir in verse, a this-is-what-happened-to-me book, although it's all there—the struggle, the necessary patience, the frustration, the successes. No, this collection is an unabashed love letter, a love letter to literature and the power of art. Generous and inclusive, Barker opens up her classroom, pushes back the walls, to reach out to anyone who ever opened a book, who trembled by the tracks with Anna Karenina; who understands, in some hiding place in the brain, Frost's "dark and deep" and the stopgap rationalization of "miles to go before I sleep." What Barker shows in these finely crafted and honest poems is what literature still has the power to do despite sound bites, commercials, political spin, and all the distortions of language we live with. At base, reading down through layers of Barker's insight, remembrance, and even confession, these poems and the literature they examine affect everyone. In this classroom, no one is exempt. Not the students, not the reader, and—bless her—not the teacher.

—Alice Friman

I Hate Telling People I Teach English

Like last August, after they'd finished my bone scan,
    this combed-over mid-sixties guy starts chatting about the novel
he's written in his head, he only needs someone like me
    to work it up, he never liked punctuation, parts of speech, all that junk
from junior high, and I couldn't get my print-out fast enough
    to take to my GP, who likes to quote from his inspirational speeches
to local luncheon clubs. He's determined to collect them
    in a book, though he'd need a good editor, do I know any, and meanwhile
I've been waiting fifty-seven minutes for help with recharging
    my sluggish thyroid, and I haven't met any doctors who like giving
free advice about your daughter's milk allergy or your friend's
    migraines or the thumb you slammed in the stairwell door, splitting it
open so badly your students interrupted your lecture on
    pronoun agreement to note you were dripping blood from your hand
and wow, what happened? But it's mostly at parties I hate
    admitting I teach English. I've never been quick enough to fudge,
the way a Methodist minister friend says he's in "support
    services" so he doesn't get called to lead grace. I guess I could dub myself
a "communications facilitator," but since I'm in the business
    of trying to obviate obfuscation, I own up, though I dread what I know
is coming: "Oh," they say, "I hated English, all that grammar,
    you won't like the way I talk, you'll be correcting me," and suddenly
they need another Bud or merlot or they've got to check out
    the meatballs or guacamole over on the table and I'm left facing
blank space, no one who can even think about correcting
    my dangling participles. Once when the computer guy was at the house,
bent over my laptop trying to get us back online,
    he asked what it was I wrote, and when I told him "poetry," said, "Ah—
fluffy stuff," and I wasn't sure whether he was kidding
    or not, but I figured at least it was better than his saying he hated poetry
or that he had a manuscript right outside in his Camry and
    could I take a look, no hurry, but he knew it would sell, could I tell him
how to get an agent for his novel about his uncle
    moving to Arizona and running a thriving ostrich farm until the day
hot-air balloons took off a half mile away

and stampeded the birds, till all he was left with were feathers and bloody
tangled necks on fence posts, the dream of making two million
       from those birds a haunting sentence fragment—but then, I think:
I would never have wanted to miss the time a dentist,
       tapping my molars, asked if I'd like to hear him recite Chaucer's Prologue
to *The Canterbury Tale*s in Middle English, which he did
       while I lay back in his chair, open-mouthed, pierced to the root.

Truth, Beauty, and the Intro Poetry Workshop

Still prickling from a neighbor's yelling "Shove it
                                    up your ass" when all I'd done was ask if
                    he could stop his terriers
from yapping all night, I wasn't entirely patient when
                                    the kid with the scarab tattoos effused about
                    beauty, said ever since Brit Lit
he's wanted to talk like Milton—"Yet once more, O ye
                                    Laurels"—or Keats—"Those lips, O slippery
                    blisses, twinkling eyes," adding
he's in the class to "build the lofty rhyme." I reminded him
                                    it's 2010, we don't wear cravats or corsets and
                    nobody waltzes anymore. He nodded,
so I asked what music he likes. "Deathcore—It Dies Today
                                    and Suicide Silence," he said, and then,
                    "I'm a drummer." "Aha," I said,
"how about writing a poem the way you wield those sticks." Now
                                    he's turned in a free-verse sequence leaded
                    with expletives about arguments
with his crack-dealing brother who never leaves the house without
                                    his .38. His lines reverberate with the turbulence
                    of a 747 out of LAX. Yet I'm
lashing myself, worrying I did him wrong. I love Auden's
                                    call to "Let the healing fountain start" from
                    "the deserts of the heart,"
but why not water this kid's land-mine-loaded sand
                                    dunes with a little harmony? The human soul
                    needs beauty more
than bread, said Lawrence. Haven't I been yearning for a bit
                                    of old-school beauty myself? Just last week
                    we watched a tennis princess
swear she'd take her fuckin' ball and slam it down the fuckin'
                                    judge's throat. I know poetry's got to breathe
                    with the fumes of its time,

but I'd like to escape my own, forget about drugged-up

                                    kids with guns. And it isn't even true nobody

                waltzes anymore. How

could I have forgotten that night downtown a year ago

                         when, as the symphony in the outdoor pavilion

                lilted into "The Blue Danube,"

a thousand people all joined in, arms lifting to arms,

                         lovers and uncles, grandmas and bikers, moms

                and toddlers dancing

under the moon to soaring melodies barely heard these days,

                         till we became one rhapsodic, dactylic swirl.

Emily in the Classroom

Hovers at the ceiling's buzzing
　　　　　fluorescent lights. The students crack
their paperbacks, pressing
　　　　　the valves of her phrases, working them
like bellows, determined
　　　　　to ignite a fire with compacted air, evade
the cold that could razor the tops
　　　　　of our heads. They want to illuminate
the shadowy dashes, the slivered
　　　　　chasms, seal them for safe-keeping
under glass. She hovers
　　　　　at the ceiling like an unfamiliar freckled
moth, like Jehovah—Yahweh—
　　　　　a name we cannot speak aloud. She is
hovering like a breath taken
　　　　　further and further until released,
a slip of thread lifted
　　　　　by the wind. If only they could spread
their feathers, gain an arc,
　　　　　know how neighborly, the invisible.

His Eyelashes Are Not Tarantulas

But I've been bitten, stung, and I want to tell this guy, star pitcher
                on the university team—bare
        arms so muscular I'm amazed
any straight woman around this table can utter a word—I'd like to shred
                his printout and toss the pieces into
        the nearest recycle bin. His poem
begins with a guy who's salivating for a "she" who's lolling her curves
                on his kitchen counter, but when the "I"
        licks and nibbles "her" moist flesh,
we learn "she" is only an apple. How do I count the ways I could sneer
                his poem's fouled out? The students
        are chuckling, "great humor," Adrian's
saying, but I'm struggling to calm down, behave like the mature workshop
                leader I'm supposed to be while my mind
        races like a runner stealing
third. I'm hurled back fifty-some years to my first steady boyfriend,
                the one I even thought about marrying,
        record-breaking pitcher on
our high school team, black lashes, eyes dark as Medjool dates. This kid
                looks just like that boy. Something very sexy
        about a pitcher—I'd sit behind
home plate—the ball coming right at me after the long wind up, intense
                crouch over the mound. He made it
        to the majors, the Braves, and once
I saw him pitch against Willie McCovey. I'd love to watch my student
                in action. I saw the old boyfriend last
        summer, after all these years, and
over lunch, without a smile, he reminded me I'd dumped him not once
                but twice. He'd never forgiven me, his back
        rigid as a Louisville Slugger while
he insisted on paying the bill. Or was he bored and eager to leave? When
                was it students began to see me as old enough
        to be their mother? That September

afternoon Marissa said in my office, "Oh Dr. Barker, your shoes are
                adorable, they're just like the ones my mom
      wears!" Now the apple arcs from
another direction—Belinda says maybe the poem's about sadness over
                a woman's desertion, so all the man's left with
      is one apple on the countertop. But—
I'll admit it—though this kid could be my grandson, he's so damned cute
                I'm smitten and all too aware I've been
      dropped from the team. Where is
that smooth-skinned girl my boyfriend loved? Forget the snide remarks
                I'd wanted to make, the rant about
      Rossetti's *Goblin Market* with
those leering men offering fruit so tongue-luscious you grew addicted,
                sickened, died. Forget my desire to snipe
      that women are not grapes, plums
waiting for hornets, yellow jackets, to sting them dry. So I tell him
                to read Shakespeare, write a new poem
      showing a lover as nothing like
a piece of fruit—and add that he'd throw a three-pitch strike-out
                if he just described an apple
      so we'd hanker for its tang.

Waking Over *Call It Sleep*

I'm the closest thing to Jewish in the class even though
at best I'm only one-eighth, according
    to my English mother, who insisted the shadowy figure
of her granny was a Jew since nobody knew
    her origins and everybody talked as if something had been
hushed up, shameful, and of course
    everything about her hawk-nosed face was unusually dark,
especially the ringlets of her unruly hair,
    or I suppose you could count the fact that I'm married
to a man whose grandparents arrived
    at Ellis Island from what is now Ukraine only three years
after Henry Roth, yet none of these
    students has the *seykhl* to know their teacher is a *shiksa*
and our group is as goyish as pork chops
    but they've all been children, and they love this novel,
they know what it's like to be
    speechless, powerless, afraid. Nobody needs me to explain
the terror of what lies beyond
    the front door and what lies within, and the paralysis
that comes from never knowing
    when to dash outside or stand by the window behind
the blinds. One year, while we were reading
    Ginsberg, I knew I'd have to describe Kaddish
though I'd never even heard it
    recited, but I gave it a go, saying in passing that only
1% of our city's population is Jewish
    which was when Heather quipped: "Of course, they're all
in Hollywood making millions from
    trashy movies." I put down my book and didn't move—
you could hear the whirr
    of the elevator down the hall. When I spoke, I said, "That
was a very offensive comment"—and
    I realized I was shaking, after decades of holding forth
in linoleum-floored classrooms. It wasn't
    like the times I've heard someone saying *wet* meaning

wetback which are both despicable

terms and I argue those too, but this time it was as if
I'd been slapped full in the face, called

sheeny, kike, and I swear that tears came to my eyes though
I couldn't cry out "*Gevalt*, help,

take that back, you ignorant little bitch." The tension lasted
beyond the ten-minute break, which

I loosened to twenty, and not just for the smokers. Now
I've handed out maps that highlight

Galicia, Brooklyn, Tysmenicz, the Lower East Side,
Avenue D, and 9th Street, and a list with

explanations of terms: Passover, Ashkenazi, knish, shul,
and pogrom. We talk about Friday night

and the candles, and everyone is right there in the room
with Roth and with me and with my husband

who joins us after the break to tell about the author's
life with his duck farm and his goyish wife

and his writer's block, and I begin to wonder if any of these
students with family from Monterrey or

Laredo will some day learn—as a friend of mine did last year—
that a great-great-great-and-beyond

grandfather came over from Spain to escape the Inquisition,
and if it will happen—as my friend Raul

told me it did—that in the lighting of candles with relatives
gathered for a first Shabbat, an elderly aunt

in the corner will begin to sigh and to weep, and when they
press her, ask her what's wrong,

she'll tell them she's suddenly remembering an abuela
who covered her face with her hands

every Friday night to greet the Divine, the Shekhinah,
and who every week sent one grandchild

to buy candles. A child, I'm thinking, who wore a silver
cross around her neck and had never

heard *judía de mierda* hurled in her face with the auto-pilot
contempt of the six girls who chanted

at me in the bathroom once during second grade, as they
pointed at the color of my striped
    dress: "Blue, blue, you're a Jew," but I didn't get it—
I thought they were saying *jewel*.

I'd Said It Would Be

Depressing, and in fact I dreaded it, hadn't even requested it,
an entire course on 19th Century literature by women. We'll feel
corseted, starved for breath, I warned on the first day,
and sure enough, after *Jane Eyre, Goblin Market, Uncle Tom's Cabin,*
and *Incidents in the Life of a Slave Girl,* when we come to Alcott's
Little Women, the whole class sighs in relief to read about Jo,
loping like an unfettered colt down the road, chomping apples
in the attic with a rat. Claudia says she liked the way Winona Rider
wore Converse high-tops to create an authentic
athletic bounce in the film with Susan Sarandon who—everyone
agrees—was not our idea of Marmee, the mother we all wish had been
ours, who never lost it, never flew off the handle
and screamed at a daughter for spilling a glass of milk. But then
Holly reminds us that Marmee confessed to Jo she'd been angry
every single day of her life. She'd kept it inside,
pushed it in, just as those corsets pressed hard on a woman's ribs,
constricted the lungs, the intestines. Liveliest discussion of the whole
semester. Though am I the only one who never
identified with Jo, but with Meg, fretting about clothes? All this
week I've been poring over catalogs, pondering whether I could risk
one of those gauzy, swirly skirts everybody's wearing now. Yesterday,
shopping for new bras, I grew dizzy wandering through racks
of styles and almost all of them gel-filled or molded so that,
trying them on, I felt like two Wagnerian breastplates
had been glued to my chest, and I couldn't get out of there
fast enough, once again lamenting the passing of the '60s, when
we happily flopped around under our blouses, free
at last. How is it, then, that while every woman in this room
proclaims her sisterhood with Jo, I'm facing a barrage of breasts
bulging from lacey camisoles and push-up bras in this
roomful of moussed, streaked and unstreaked, upswept and
downswept spiral-curled locks of hair? Here we are, in
the twenty-first century, and we're still obsessing,

jittery, even frantic about judgments from the telescopic

lenses of the world beyond our closet door. The Academy

Awards focus less on the arts of acting and

cinematography than on Penelope Cruz's "white embellished

strapless gown" with its "luscious satin folds." I won't ask

how long Claudia takes to do her hair so it lifts a hillock

over her head and then drops like a waterfall, an auburn-

streaked cascade. As long, I'd think, as it took to arrange

Marianne Dashwood's looped-up ringlets in *Sense*

and Sensibility. I know the '90s ushered in the era of Girl Power,

and I'm not the sort of second-wave feminist who'll be

buried in her Birkenstocks, but I doubt we've made

that much progress when our guys slouch around all comfy

in tee-shirts and baggy jeans. I guess one of those swirly skirts

might look okay on me, as long as I wore opaque

stockings, hid my varicose shins. How I wish we could break

out of this whale-boned century and move on, at least

to the twentieth. Fast forward to Harjo, gallop

like horses of "fur and teeth," horses that burn like stars. Strip

down to hard, unadorned muscle and flesh, wade into Lucille

Clifton's poems, shake ungirdled hips with "space

to move around in." But we're laced tight to the syllabus, and

the only way out is for Jane Eyre to marry her Rochester,

for Jo March to wed Professor Bhaer, her "bear,"

after learning to bite her "abominable tongue." How long

before someone, anyone in this room, will begin to growl?

In the Seminar, Trying to Launch *Passage to India*

I've got to lecture on Forster and the Raj, the partition of Bengal,
                 but I can't focus, and it's not only
         that I'm remembering my own months
in India, the smells of cardamom, turmeric mingling with charcoal
                 smoke amid rickshaws, water
         buffalo, bicycles, camels, and eighteen
wheelers. It's that I'm still twitchy about the Englishness I inherited
                 from my mother, who sailed
         to New York from Southampton
on the Queen Mary. So when Lisa complains the novel is confusing,
                 she can't keep track of the weird
         names, I push my notes aside. "Okay,"
I say, "Let's make a list, start with the Brits." "Hopeless," spouts Richard,
                 "they're racists, all of them, imperialist
         capitalists using their hegemonic power
to oppress the indigenous people. Detestable, disgusting, especially
                 Miss Quested," he grumbles. I've been
         dealing with my Anglophobia
for years, ashamed of the way my mother and her snobbish brother
                 would blithely butcher names
         of places, saying "Urnuhk*oo*lum"
instead of "Ern*a*kulam," with the emphasis on the wrong syllable. But
                 before I can ask if everyone in the class
         found *all* the Brits in the novel
despicable, Lupita asks why they have to live off by themselves
                 on the hill. "Because they like
         playing royalty," sneers Richard,
adding, "They're recreating their own little England with their canned
                 peas and their stupid plays." He's
         right. Yet I can't forget my third day
in Delhi, when Manjit led me into the sudden calm of the Hyatt
                 and fed me a lemon lassi, saying
         she could see I'd been about to
go under from too much India too fast. And I'd thought myself
                 the consummate traveler—a dozen

stamps on my passport. I won't
mention the time on the beach south of Chennai when a horde
of kids followed me, clutching
at my kameez till I broke free
and stumbled into an Anglican church with its pews lined up
in rows. If it had been
1920, with a pink-cheeked British
officer nearby, I could have blubbered about those hateful boys
taunting and poking, could have
created as big a crisis as Adela Quested
when she accuses Aziz of accosting her in the cave. Now Marcy
is asking what the British were
doing in India anyway, and I've
got to backtrack to Elizabeth I, tea, opium, and indigo. But I hear
the fluting voice of my English
granny, a governess in the Punjab
who regretted the return to London, where she missed the neem
trees, the banyans, the spices,
the Bhatnagar family, and the bulbul's
song. "So what happened in the Malabar Caves," Annie is asking,
and Cathy answers: "Before Adela
entered the cavern, she was
Ronny Heaslop's fiancée, but inside the cave, she heard the voice
of her real self, so when she
came out, she'd changed,
just like India changed him, he's not the same guy she knew
in England, he's turned into
a bureaucratic jerk." And Michael
adds that, "After Adela left the cave, she heard an echo in her ear till
she finally confesses Aziz had
never bothered her at all." I didn't
know, when I arrived at JFK's Gate B31 for my first flight to Delhi,
my eyes the only blue ones among
hundreds slouched in plastic

chairs, waiting to board, that when I returned home I'd be headed
                              for a divorce. And I didn't
            know, in towns like Ludhiana,
some men knew American women only from TV, believed us
                    all to be sluts, so I was half
        embarrassed and half flattered
at the dinner party where the guy kept snuggling up, calling me
                    Marilyn Monroe, me with my
            breasts no bigger than dollops of dal,
with my gray-blond hair, while my horrified elegant hosts
                        pried him away. But now
        I'm telling the students how
I learned to say "atcha" in Punjabi, the one word I was sure I could
                    master, trying over and over until,
            furious at my inability even to pronounce
the word for "okay," I lost it, blew up, hissed, snorted "uh-*chah*"
                    as loud as I could, and the whole
            room shouted, I'd done it, I'd gotten it,
I could almost pass for Punjabi. Now even Richard is laughing. Yet
                        I don't mention how angry
        I really was, how exhausted, frustrated,
and, unlike Adela Quested, up to my neck in "the real India,"
                    even though people were
            oh, so kind, exclaiming how well
I was managing for my first time. The fluorescent lights begin
                        their erratic, crackling hum,
            and Lisa catches my eye,
plunges in: "Mrs. Moore got it, didn't she, she liked sitting with Aziz
                    in the temple, he even
            praised her by saying she was
'Oriental,' but why did she freak out in the caves?" Cathy explains
                        that "Mrs. Moore had trusted
            people's goodness, but
inside the cave, all her old beliefs are erased. And see how on page 223
                    Forster says Mrs. Moore wasn't

the 'dear old lady' everyone
thought, India 'brought her into the open.'" Michael, José, and
                          Annie are nodding. Marcy is
          jotting notes. I give it a minute,
take a long breath. "You know," I say, "we're all tired. What if
                    we quit for now. I'll see you
          next week." But before I let them go—
I can't stop myself—I tell them about the first night I ever spent
                    in India, when the lock
          to my room at the Delhi
YWCA wouldn't open from the inside, and my friends kept calling,
                    but the phone didn't work
          and I couldn't figure out
how to let them know I was trapped until the clerk at the desk
                    agreed to break the rules
          and allow my frantic
university hosts to climb the stairs and bang on my door, holler
                    at me, *"Are you there? Are you there?"*
          like a blinding echo, and
I wasn't even sure if I was, or when I got out, who I would be.

About That "One Art"

It's a perfect poem, I say, and though no one
　　　　　　　in the class is over twenty-five, everybody
nods. They've all lost: the Madame
　　　　　　　Alexander doll fallen into the toilet, silky
hair never the same, the friend who
　　　　　　　moved away to Dallas, a brother once again
in juvie. So many schools—thirteen in
　　　　　　　a dozen years—I lost each friend I made
till grad school. And every move since,
　　　　　　　something always missing—this last time,
the box that held my photo albums
　　　　　　　of the sixties, that elastic, unveined life I'd
love to visit just once more. And now
　　　　　　　the husbands of so many have diminished—
the cancerous prostates, the double
　　　　　　　bypasses, the radiation, the chemo. One died
while napping. And how many women friends
　　　　　　　have lost a breast? Or two? Now I wonder,
who'll be leaving first: me, or you? Just how
　　　　　　　will that be mastered? And how is it even time
begins to lose itself? In class I ask why Bishop
　　　　　　　wrote the poem as a villanelle, and so we
parse the form, say how such echoing
　　　　　　　slows us, keeps us focused on each single
disappearance, so at first we hear lightheartedness,
　　　　　　　a witty irony—but then the sounds grow
vaster, catch us off guard. And quicken.

Teaching *Mrs. Dalloway* I'm Thinking

How I'd like to buy flowers, how I'd like to place a sterling
      silver bowl of peonies or cut-glass vase of tulips and irises
on the laminate seminar table in this windowless room,
      and I'm thinking how I'd like to arrive before the one student
always a half-hour early, how I'd like to greet each of them
      at the door, inquire after their sisters and cousins, their tíos
and abuelitas, and comfort the one who's been fired
      from his job. Every Tuesday another novel about the modern
condition, those catchy phrases we use: "alienation
      and fragmentation"—while for the past three weeks Jill,
the debate team captain on two scholarships, hasn't said
      a word because, she told me sobbing at the break, her boyfriend
was found bloody in his apartment, shot by her brother
      off his meds, and Angie, dispatching for Pleasure U Hot Line,
her shift moved to graveyard, slumps dozing
      in her chair. Now Jeffrey is saying, "She's snobbish, Clarissa,
I don't like her, who cares about her maids and
      her flowers, but she's right, I mean, she gets it, nothing like
a great party." It's the dinner hour, though no bells chime
      on this campus, and only two of us have actually heard Big Ben,
have ever strolled through Regent's Park, ridden on
      a red double-decker. But nobody around this table wonders
why Septimus hurls himself out the window, nobody
      needs PTSD explained, and when Marita asks, "Wasn't it Woolf
who filled her pockets with stones and walked into
      a river?" nobody says "weird," their two dozen heads bent over
pages littered with post-its. I'm thinking how I want
      to say something, mend this rent in the air the way Clarissa
gathers the raveled threads of her ripped dress with a needle,
      the way she draws everyone into her party, but already it's time
to pack up our pens, our notebooks, head out on the crowded
      interstate, past all the newly constructed buildings with no
balconies, no wrought iron railings, these multiple stories
      of steel and glass, mirrored so no one can see into them.

Alone In the Museum's Greek Collection

Of course I'm reminded of "Ode on a Grecian
      Urn," and wonder if, next fall when I teach Keats again,
            I could bring the class to peer through all this glass
                  at the dozens of amphorae on their crisp laminate
stands. Amphora: from the Greek "to bear." And
      how these urns bear up, carry sketches of a life we can
            barely conjure, the pregnant middles of these glossy
                  vessels displaying such slender, muscular boys, heroes,
goddesses—and the Furies. But I fear I'd ignore
      the students—I'd be mesmerized—as I am now—by an urn
            labeled "Attic Red-Figure Column-Krater." Here's Orestes
                  kneeling on a pile of rocks, head bowed to the winged
Fury on his left, snakes writhing round
      her arms. He's just killed his mother and her lover,
            revenge for their slaying his father. His body is contorted,
                  knees and feet turned toward Apollo and Artemis, who
stand opposite, as if to offer solace. He seems
      almost ripped in half. The way judges might absolve us,
            saying "rightful cause," or a minister, reminding us we're
                  only human, and yet we're chased for years, threatened
with all the Furies' snakes. I think of the words
      I muttered in the doorway of the room where
            my mother lay dying, hurtful words she may have heard,
                  and of the words I couldn't say during the days before
my father died. There was the time I shook
      and shook my colicky infant son and screamed
            into his tiny face when he'd been crying for hours
                  and nothing I'd done could soothe him—his shrieks
shifted then to terror. Those Furies still
      know where to find me, hurling their hissing vipers
            around my shoulders. Though Aeschylus tells us Orestes
                  will be absolved, there's no release shown on this jar,
his body twisting at the core. Families—
      the wars within that shape the wars without. How
            can our deeds be laid to rest? Ripples in perpetuity.

On Teaching Too Many Victorian Novels in Too Short a Space
of Time During Which I Become

Stuffed, like a twenty-pound turkey crammed to the crust-slithery maw
not with croutons and giblets, but ribbons, pendants, waistcoats, ruffles, and plumes
till I'm dazed, logy, needing a nap trying to keep track during eight hundred
pages of Bulstrodes, Cadwalladers, Featherstones, Chicheleys, Plymdales, Hackbutts,
and Minchins, when those English villages didn't hold as many people as I pass
on the interstate in fifteen minutes or dodge at the mall the day after Thanksgiving
or slump down with at the gate waiting for the delayed flight or stare at on CNN
or MSNBC in an hour, surfing through head after talking head, each expounding
to me lounging on my couch as though we were all seated around a mahogany table
loaded with glistening plate and leaded goblets, embossed napkins, and candelabras.
But the sixteen of us at five metal-legged tables jigsawed together in our department's
closet of a seminar room, with no possibility of pushing back chairs, leaning into pillows,
gazing into a fire, and holding to the light a snifter of cognac the color of autumn
leaves somewhere in an English village, are chatting away as though we are neighbors,
as if the characters in *Middlemarch* lived next door, and we've become vicar, solicitor,
seamstress, and a cousin all rolled into one, as we analyze Dorothea's encumbered vistas,
Lydgate's tightening financial noose—how lonely, how restricted, we say, grateful
for the roominess, the promise of our lives, though none of us mentions our MasterCard
or Chevy Avalanche payments, just as we ignore the fact that few of us have met
our own neighbors, since nobody ever asks anybody over for tea or drinks or Scrabble,
and if somebody is burgled or shot, we might hear about it on the car radio
driving home after Monday's six o'clock class, another night without dinner.

Rereading *The Golden Bowl*

I'd rather carry my grandmother's iridescent
      Tiffany vase across six rutted parking lots while rolling
my briefcase and gripping my lunch than teach this
      book. When it comes to the Master, I want to keep him
to myself, thread my own way through
      polished drawing rooms and twisting garden paths. I'd
rather feel that if I'm hanging fire, speechless
      in the middle of class, musing over Maggie's ruminations
to Fanny—all those suspicions about her
      husband and her father's wife—I can pause as long as
I'd like. When Grandma's vase crashed
      from the table, I was never sure whether the neighbor's
elbow had jostled it or my German shepherd's
      tail. Two months after I'd rescued it from my cousin's
garage sale, potter friends explained
      what the etched *L.C.T.* on the bottom meant, and then,
the next day, it shattered. We live our
      lives through objects, I've heard an artist say. I glued
the fragments, a crude joining, but
      the best I could do. All the flaws, visible and invisible,
within marriages. Friends of a woman I love
      keep urging her to dump her imperious husband of forty
years. But once, when I dropped her off after
      a Woody Allen film, before I pulled out of the drive,
I saw her through the front door's oval glass
      with that potbellied man, an embrace so tender, so rapt,
I wanted to stay right there in my car in the dark,
      absorb some of that closeness. How do we ever know
what goes on between any couple? Why
      people stay, or wriggle free, or bolt? Maggie's husband
seems every inch a prince, though we begin
      to wonder. Then we question our wondering. I'm finally
having Grandma's vase restored, by a woman
      who understands glass. She says when she's finished
we'll barely see the gaps missing their

minuscule shards. Favrile—its color shifts as you turn it
in the light, violet to green to blue and

rose. A technique Tiffany patented in 1894, ten years
before the novel. It's not that

Maggie really lied, but that her subtle phrasings mended
her marriage—in the end, everyone was

"magnificent." For Henry James, broadcasting naked
truths would rip the webbing that holds

the world in place. I'll never teach *The Golden Bowl*—
even grad students might insist on finding

a single culprit, or demand an outburst, somewhere
in those labyrinthine paragraphs,

of uncorseted, unchaperoned emotion. Despite my
awkward gluing job, the fluted edges

of that vase lifted for all those years like petals, satiny
as the hems fluttering around

Grandma's nylon-stockinged legs that tottered under
the weight of far too many whiskeys

while she held my hand, stroked my hair, and called me
precious. Melting together various colors

of glass causes the opalescence of favrile. There's an
exercise I like to give in writing

workshops: Imagine you're holding an heirloom vase
in your hands. Turn it around, feel its shape,

its smooth or grainy, pebbly texture. Now look down
into it, where at the bottom you'll see

a wisp of thread or a hairline crack. Which is it? What
happens next? Maybe in time

one student will find a tattered copy of the book, will
open it with a careful hand, so

the pages won't crumble, the spine doesn't break.

Wang Wei in the Workshop

Twelve hundred years
since the eighth century.
Of nineteen translations,
we've looked at five.
Lily is crying after
reading her poem
about her home city
of Hong Kong, where,
in a building designed
for ten dozen stories,
six men hauling waste
died when the elevator
shaft collapsed and
plunged twenty floors.
From that roof, no one
sees the house
of a small family
eating from porcelain
bowls on a wooden
table balanced
on level ground.
How can a moon
slip so far down
those concrete walls?

Langston Hughes' "Weary Blues"

Needs no explaining in this class. No one needs a gloss
                on "Suicide's Note," that river so calm, asking a kiss,
      yet none of us around this table
                has ever been kept out of a KFC or a multiplex
because of our skin. "Nobody knows the trouble
                I've seen," sang Lena Horne, who couldn't stay
      at the Savoy-Plaza after she'd
                made the crowd swing. Enough trouble right here
in this room. Ann's just driven from the hospice,
                her gay dad's body shriveling into the sheets,
      her mother and brothers refusing
                to visit. Last week Robert's cousins were found
mangled by the train tracks in Sabinas for the Los Zetas
                dope they were running, only way to pay for beans
      and rice. This morning in my office
                Christina soaked through the six tissues I offered
as she told how the fucked-up ex-marine raped her
                in the ass over and over, his loaded .45 beside
      the pillow. No wonder Hughes'
                pianist "stopped playing and went to bed," where
he "slept like a rock or a man that's dead." I need
                to focus on the poem, call and response, structure
      of the blues. Nathan might help,
                he's a musician. But already he's talking: "Hey, after
class, how many of y'all want to drive over to JJ's, awesome
                piano, sax, bass." And all I say is, "Count me in."

Why I Dread Teaching *The Sun Also Rises*

When I used to picture the whole class, all fifty-six of us, lounging
        around a bar, sprawled under a fly-ridden
fan creaking overhead with a bartender listening like a burnt-out priest
        and a throaty half-lidded alto crooning to a mike,
I'd forget that always, even after I deliver my riff about World War One
        and life in the trenches where the guys
watched their buddies' brains explode into bloody pulp after wading
        for months in mud up to their knees,
one of the students, maybe Tiffany, will begin to whine, "This book
        is disgusting, why should we care about no-good
drunks wandering around destroying their God-given bodies,
        and as for Brett, she's a total slut, the fact
that Jake loves her tells you how sick he is, and anyway, why do we
        have to read such depressing novels?"
Then Bryan will say, "Yeah, she's right, and how come these dudes
        can afford to eat in all these pricey restaurants,"
and even after William chimes in to counter that Jake actually has a job,
        Bryan will sneer, "Sure, he works maybe five minutes
between drinks"—and it's uphill work to steer the class back on track,
        ask them if they've ever been hurt so badly
all they want to do is forget, but if I'm lucky it'll be William who pipes up
        again to say, "Haven't y'all done Fiesta, come on,
you know how you party nonstop till you find out which of your friends
        are the real jerks, the serious assholes, and
then you know the score, aren't fooled by anybody any more." Maybe
        I used to remember the year when I traveled
with a cousin and his group of musicians, summer afternoons in Verona
        over a three-hour lunch before the concert
when the notes of Vivaldi flew to the dome of the cathedral and lived
        in my ears all the next day and the next as we ordered
Campari and soda before the evening's *passegiatta*, the long lounging
        at a round table as we watched the women and men
saunter and the *ragazzi* jostle and the swallows lift above the piazza,
        swirl and dip while the sun dropped and the sky

turned rose, before a few of us found a little *ristorante* and ordered trout
        caught that morning from a stream in the Dolomites
where later we walked in meadows so far above the cars and smoke
        we thought we'd been lofted to a snow-glazed heaven.
During those months I forgot everything but the sweet tang of the air.
        But that's not the whole of it, not really the truth.
How I worked to forget the nights when that cousin was so drunk
        he made Mike in the novel look like a hero,
made Frances' sniping at Robert Cohn look sweet and kind, the way
        he'd yell at his girlfriend and call her "bitch,"
the way his hands would slide over the breasts and bottoms of women
        before they even realized he'd crossed that boundary
right out in public, and why nobody slugged him I still don't know.
        But then there was the semester when Guadalupe
perked up the class by saying that the novel reminded her of childhood
        in Monterrey, when her father took the family
to the Plaza de Toros on Sundays and explained why the *torero* wears
        a suit of lights decorated with gold and silver threads,
and how he uses the long skinny sword only for killing, how it's all a ritual,
        and that—just like Jake tells Brett—you're supposed
to focus on the bull, on every little movement, so it's not so horrible,
        it's like a ballet, a dance, though with death, and
so graceful it's kind of beautiful, but even so, she found it hard to see
        all the blood, and hardest to watch the horses.
The students were lined up in rows of unmoveable desks, and
        one of the fluorescent bulbs overhead
flickered on and off as the room grew quiet and nobody rustled a page.
        It's not so easy to spot grace under pressure.
I always wanted to be one of the insiders—not a whiner,
        sentimental, squeamish, like Robert Cohn.
When I taught *Lord of the Flies* to high school seniors, a couple of boys
        brought in a bloody pig's head dripping
in a paper bag, and I only said, "Cool, where did you guys get that?"
        These days I can't stomach anything stronger
than San Pellegrino after years as a Johnny Walker on the rocks

wannabe aficionado, and I've never been in a war.
But I know how it feels when someone in a group, even in a family,
       goes berserk like a maddened bull, how it feels when
from out of nowhere, talk fired like a mortar shell explodes the head
       sitting next to you, maybe your own, open
down to the bone, with no one who can bring together the viscous
       edges of the wound, and you're so numb
all you can do is try to walk without stumbling, focus on the next step,
       the next drink, even if it's orange juice, because
this bull won't give up the ghost with a straight swoop of a blade.
       What you want is to go off alone and dive
into deep, clean water, start over with no carnage anywhere in sight,
       as if you could, and isn't it pretty to think so.

Whenever We've Dipped into *Walden*

Some sophomore will say "Sure, okay, I get Thoreau's
                 whole 'tonic of wildness' thing, but it's not so noble
        to live off by yourself with the beavers,"
and I'll almost agree, till I remember sailing through
                 Norwegian fjords with a hankering to live out my days
        gazing at larches and spruce, whirling
gulls and waterfalls. Those inlets more pristine than
                 Squam, the New Hampshire lake where I splashed
        in the shallows before I could walk. But
living alone on a sub-arctic slope, I'd shrivel to a brittle
                 husk. Not only Squam's dappling birch leaves, expanse
        of water beyond the pine needles
clustered in bundles snug as my sisters and me tucked in
                 our cots—we had those silvery nights and days together,
        no alarms jangling us awake and
shoving us off to separate schools in buses crammed with
                 jostling kids. We didn't know then how often Grandpop
        bellowed at Daddy after breakfast
or that Grandma drank herself dizzy before dinner,
                 didn't know why Mom ignored speed limits careening
        into Plymouth for aspirin and
more sherry. Nightmares never infected our sleep
                 in the cottage where ancestors had dressed to be married,
        no naggings interrupted our Nestlé's
cocoa in the high-raftered hall beside the field where our
                 great-uncles' horseshoes clanked before Vespers. Invisible,
        our dead, like rings inside the white
pines. My sisters and I bestowed secret names on every
                 granite boulder we climbed. But over the years we drifted,
        driven by calendars and deadlines,
by fears of Mom's sporadic rages, Daddy's withdrawals, hissed
                 breaths, the jangling ice in his highballs. And our jealousies:
        which of us was prettiest, smartest,

nicest, which one Mom prized most. "We do not treat ourselves
           nor one another thus tenderly," said Thoreau. Yet now after
     funerals and weddings, divorces,
remarriages, after a son-in-law's suicide, a brother's multiple
           myeloma, we've returned to the lake. During class, one
     student will always remind us
that Henry David didn't exactly make it on his own
           while squatting on Emerson's land, since friends stopped by
     to talk about books, his mother
brought him fresh-baked blueberry pies, and he'd stroll
           into the village for gossip and cornmeal. How could I
     "suck out all the marrow of life"
if I were alone? By that New Hampshire lake, the past rests
           underfoot like pine needles softening to silt. Last June,
     after the semester's end, when my sisters
and I returned to Squam, while they were off with husbands
           and kids, canoeing or napping on the porch or finishing
     another 3000-piece puzzle, a familial quiet
pillowed the granite stone I leaned on, formed from the earth's
           magma how many eons ago, those volcanic eruptions
     that solidified into the rockbed
holding me to one small ridge, one ripple in a vast open
           bowl, the lake where water is always leaving to become air.

Preparing Jeffers' "Vulture" Before Class

I'm already predicting the reaction: "Who cares 'how beautiful
        he looked,' that bird gliding 'on those great sails,'
                this guy is freaking weird
if he wants to be shredded like that." So I'm wondering if I should
        mention what happened a year ago when
                I turned from a booth on
wind power at our neighborhood's GreenFest to face a Eurasian
        Eagle Owl on a man's gloved arm. Stared right
                into me. I don't know
how long I froze, swept into that centered gaze. I guess tonight
        I could propose that maybe death Jeffers' way
                wouldn't be worse than
the doctors' slipping a gastric feeding tube into my father's
        stomach, puncturing his lung, then jamming
                a ventilating tube down
his throat, after which he never talked again. "Iatrogenic mishaps,"
        such things are called, the complications, side
                effects of common medical
procedures, like the euphemism "therapies" for the chiseling
        through bone, the screws in my mother's knees,
                the implanted defibrillator
that shocked her heart back to its familiar thud after it had
        wrenched to a stop. Finally she gave up eating,
                and then, even water. She'd
never read the Dylan Thomas poem, never raged against
        the dying of the light. I know what Goethe
                said, but is it really light
that leaves? I've read accounts of mystics who talk of luminosity,
        radiance that beckons, leads them to die in
                utter calm. That Eagle Owl,
its clean ferocity—a moment nothing short of rapture. No wonder
        people say those birds connect us with
                the universe. As if to scoff

at all our needles, tubes, the tinkerings, machinery we submit to,
　　　　hoping we'll delay what has to come. But
　　　　　　the vulture, Jeffers knew,
feeds only on flesh no longer living, and, even then, a social
　　　　bird, it calls to neighboring flocks to join
　　　　　　in cleaning up the land,
this bird that, for the Pueblo people, signaled purification. The Parsi
　　　　Zoroastrians exposed their dead on "towers
　　　　　　of silence," a final act
of charity, providing the birds with food that otherwise would
　　　　go to waste. *Cathartes Aura*: "Golden
　　　　　　Purifier"—in Buddhism,
compassion. Which is spacious, patient, allowing for existing
　　　　things to change. I remember reading
　　　　　　that once a toddler was
found on a mountain peak beside a vulture. He'd been missing
　　　　for three days, but was smiling, utterly
　　　　　　unhurt, though on his
grimy shirt were pierced two sets of talon marks, a rip
　　　　from a hooked beak. "What an
　　　　　　enskyment," says
Jeffers. What a way to begin a life, or, I'm thinking, end.

Innisfree, They Get

These sophomores understand a lake—or the South
                                 Texas shore, the Gulf. But they don't
             know the birds. Or plants, or flowers. Today
with Williams' poem, Queen Anne's lace has never
                                 been so remote a thing, and though
             just north of town it takes the fields by force,
these kids have never noticed. I draw
                                 an image on the board: the umbel
             and its dozens of florets. My art work's
lame, but now the flower's in focus. I say
                                 I know they've seen the grasses along
             the interstate, the way in a breeze they dip
and sway, and just imagine a whole field
                                 of these white blossoms trembling
             like a single body that quivers from simply
being touched. Last month when reading
                                 Yeats, everyone knew that primal
             longing for water, if not an Irish lake,
then the pond at an opa's hill country ranch,
                                 or the creek by an abuelo's house
             near the border. Some even knew
that Yeats' bean rows referred to *Walden*,
                                 and each one of them, I could tell
             from their eyes, wanted peace to come
dropping slow. Laptops sat inert beside
                                 that vision. But even I hadn't known
             that Yeats' linnet was not some uniquely
Irish avian creature, but close cousin
                                 to the same red house finch that flocks
             to my own feeder, perches in our live oaks
and pittosporum every day, in the deep
                                 core of my own life, where—and this
             I won't tell the students—you are with me,
day and night, the fibers of that touch,
                                 all a glimmer, and right here, at home.

I'm Not Sure the Cherry Is the "Loveliest of Trees"

So from the first line of the poem I'm quibbling,
        and I don't even teach this poem now
I'm pushing threescore and ten. All that counting
        Housman has us busy doing, figuring
the speaker's age, and I know in class we'd end up
        focusing on the stanzas with the math. Yet
students never had trouble getting hold
        of the poem's carpe diem message: inhale
the scent of roses while you can. I've never seen
        a flowering cherry, have never known
spring in Washington D.C. or England or
        been invited to a *hanami*, a party to view
the blooms in Tokyo. But I knew the dogwoods
        lacing my first hesitant steps, have known
white pines' needles gleaming with
        light reflected from a northern lake, and
I've known the palo verdes in the dusty Sonoran
        desert where Rudy, my first boyfriend,
kissed me. And the olives I planted
        with my former husband, shoveling down
into Phoenix hardpan. The eucalyptus lifting
        their astringent scent in the Berkeley hills
where I lay in a carpet of fog-softened leaves, ecstatic
        with a lover. The lemon tree by the front door
of the house where my son was born. I could say
        "with rue my heart is laden" for these and all
the trees I may never see again: banyans and teak,
        neem trees, cinnamon and coconut palms,
the bodhi tree—under which the Buddha
        sat so still. And since I haven't many springs
left in me—a dozen? two?—maybe,
        like the woman diagnosed with terminal
cancer who traveled seven continents
        compiling a life list of eight thousand birds,

I could search out all the trees I've never seen,

                        including the blossoming cherry. In California
there's a bristlecone that's lived for almost

                        five thousand years, and in Sweden, a spruce
that's lived for close to ten. That woman's travels

                        kept her cancer in remission, her doctors
were amazed. But how can I leave our own

                        Mexican persimmon near the drive, its peeling
layers of coppery silver bark, its branching

                        trunk I can't begin to wrap my arms around?

Coming to Cather

I'm still afloat from last night's performance of Mahler's Fourth,
                                and the room is strangely silent till Michele
                looks up and whispers,
"This is the best book of the semester." Everyone nods, but
                                their eyes are vague, unfocused, as if they're
                surrounded by an earthen
sea of gramas and bluestems, wading through prairie
                                grasses that once stretched from Manitoba
                down into Cather's Nebraska
and on into Texas. It's time to get the class going, but I can't
                                block out that theme from the third movement,
                the violins. A relief
when Charlotte speaks up, says her family came from the same
                                Bohemia as Ántonia's, and that her great-grandfather
                built violins, violas, and
cellos for his wife and kids, their own double string
                                quartet. She insists, "He'd never have committed
                suicide like Ántonia's dad." But
Jason says, "It could zap anybody's spirit, plowing unbroken
                                sod," and Geoffrey adds that "Ántonia's father
                was a really talented
musician, respected in the old country, so how could he
                                be a farmer, no surprise he shot himself, living
                in a dugout hovel." I hear
the strings again, the violinists' bows lifting at the same
                                moment like the grasses in a breeze, stems
                bending in one
direction. But I bring myself back to the book, and
                                we linger over lines describing the prairie grass
                that "was the country,
as the water is the sea." Years ago, moving to Texas, I felt
                                adrift as if I'd entered Cather's novel, living
                as we did on a parcel of land

out of town, no neighbors in sight. I tell the class about

                       the Polish word *tęsknota*: stronger than our

         "nostalgia," meaning "pain

of distance." The sound of those cellos in the Mahler. My then

                    husband tried to grow all our own food. Wanted

         goats, chickens, melons,

corn. Acres of land we couldn't afford, bugs, rabbits, deer,

                    hot wind biting at the garden, bad weather chewing

         on the marriage. The dogs'

tails whisked through waves of the grasses like fins. How

                   that husband filled our narrow house with music,

         sounds of his viola, silky

tenor lofting toward the trees. No human voice in Mahler's

                   Fourth till the last movement. A lone soprano

         singing of a childlike heaven. It was

a long drive into town those years, as we tried to keep the pair of

                   ourselves afloat. Only five minutes left in the class

         and I need to wrap things up,

explain next week's assignment. But I wish all twenty-two of us

                   could pile into our cars, caravan out to the hills

         where now in November

the grasses are seeding. Mahler's work begins and ends

                   in a different key. I haven't wanted to return

         to the place where the marriage

went under. Twelve, maybe fifteen years have passed

                   and finally, I hear the symphony, whole again.

The Morning After Our Second Ecopoetry Class

I'm online reading that our infant universe rang
        with reverberations of cosmic bells that rippled the primordial
    darkness like a pond pounded by stones, and I'm still
thinking about Daniel's puzzlement last night
        over the essay "Nature and Silence," in which Christopher Manes
    argues we need to listen to the language of the world
beyond our human words. But even though Melanie
        brought drawings showing how the Chinese ideogram for *bird*
    developed from an image of an actual bird, and even
though I explained that *aleph* and the letter *A*
        came from the Phoenician symbol for ox, Daniel was not alone
    in wondering how rocks could speak. We talked
for half an hour about the way words can mask,
        serve as distractions. Once, at Tortuguero, about to go zip-lining,
    six of us chattered away on the platform a hundred
and fifty feet above the rain forest floor until
        we let loose to zoom along the cable over the canopy, the kids
    whooping like howlers, those raucous monkeys whose
cries I'd mistaken for rowdies at the hotel bar
        the night before. We sped over trees so fast we couldn't have
    seen a motmot or aracari if it had flitted right below
our ankles. On the ground, our guide pointed out
        Jesus Christ lizards and spectacled caimans I might have mistaken
    for logs. He knew the calls of manakins, oropendolas,
and toucans—he would stop and cock his head
        to listen—but oh, how he would natter. Kayaking in the midst
    of mangroves thick with the absence of human prattle,
he'd be rapid-firing details about the next
        day's agenda. One midnight, four of us followed a local guy
    onto the beach, the tide thrumming its mantra
beneath a spangling of stars. It wasn't long
        before the green sea turtles dragged their four-hundred-pound
    bodies onto the beach to dig their nests. We stood

beside one as she dropped a hundred eggs down
> into the hollowed sand. Other than the rustle of surf, there was
no sound but the dry chuff, sigh, the gasp she gave
between each batch of half a dozen glistening eggs,
> the flesh within the carapace gathering strength for the next
long push. These creatures have been around
for two hundred million years. Hindus say
> it's a giant turtle that holds up the world. Next Thursday
I'll tell the class about that night, how none of us spoke,
even walking back up the beach and
> down the road. But how to describe a silence that echoes
in the rocky crust, the mantle of my bones.

Teaching "The Red Wheelbarrow" the 30th Time

I know I've explained how
         Williams didn't like tapping
tired old symbols, but
            these sophomores are
      not convinced. They've
got that wheelbarrow hard
      at work: it symbolizes life, since
it's red, like blood; they've
          got it carrying feed, back and
      forth from the coop to keep
those chickens alive so
      they can be busy laying eggs,
though they're white, which
         stands for death. Susanna
      says the poem is about
her grandpa, up at four
      and out to the barn. I'm tired
of chatter, of words dragged
         around to mean what they
      don't. I'm tired of stories,
of somebody always *doing* something, or not
      doing what somebody
wishes they would. Tired of the whole
         subject-verb-object paradigm. I'd
      even like erasing
the prepositions in the poem,
      deleting "beside" and "with." I want
only the barrow, feathers, and
         water left from rain. Separate,
      not even in relation, as
with the elements of a T'ang Dynasty poem,
      the kind Williams loved,
the sort he and
         Rexroth translated. Just
      the Chinese characters

like drawings, the blank
           spaces breaths, each one
itself: wheelbarrow, red, rain water, chickens,
                    white. There's
           a quiet I want that won't happen
in this discussion,
           a silence that comes after
long rain, the hush
                when you swear you can
           feel the swirl of
planets, the shifting
           of rocks. I should lead
the class outside; we could
                sit on the grass, look
           at a red bud
tree, an empty
           stone bench. But somehow
I end up telling a story
                after all, the one about
           Williams the doctor
having just explained to a mother and father
           their child would die, or
was it the child
                had died and
           he had to break the news. Then
he walked down
           the hall and stared out the window
at a wheelbarrow and a few
                chickens. Now
           the whole class is with me. I don't
remember where
           I heard the story. I'm not sure
it's even true. The poem itself is
                silent. You can't hear
           any clucking.

After Spring Break, Arriving at Pound's
"In a Station of the Metro"

          I'm just home from five days of slogging through
overcoats and umbrellas and feet, cold
          pavement in New York. Weary of crowds. "How can
this be a poem?" asks Jay, and—
          though for years I've loved these two lines—I hesitate,
thinking: if Pound's "Petals on a wet,
          black bough" are like faces in a crowd, they must be
wilted, bruised by the hammering
          clamor of hustle and need. "It's about ghosts," Jennifer
insists, "or at least dead people, and
          someone's putting flowers by a grave. The bough,"
she goes on, "is the casket, and the crowd's
          the family, everybody's crying, so the bough's wet
with tears." But Graciela says she knows
          they call the subway system in Paris "Le Métro," so
the poem is "a metaphor showing
          how people in the dirty underground tunnel look fresh,
like flowers." Thirty heads lift and nod,
          and for a split second I'm back in line at La Guardia's
Gate B5 waiting to buy a bottle of water,
          my carry-on slicing into my shoulder, as the faces
around me swivel like sunflowers
          toward the sun when a teenage boy whispers, "It's her,
it is, it's Halle Berry," and suddenly we're all
          abloom, a petaled row leading to one specimen
rose, even as our feet cramp
          into the tile floor. "I get it," says Molly. "This is
about the surreal feeling you'd have
          in a subway, a rush of people, and you don't know
anyone. Still, you feel every human being
          is delicate." I tell them that the poem grew after
Pound was stunned by the flood
          of faces emerging from the Métro at La Concorde,
how he struggled to compress

thirty lines into twenty seed-packed words. Molly's
right that we're ephemeral as
        flowers, and Jennifer may not be so far off after all,
for none of us—not Halle Berry, not
        this classroom, nothing, except perhaps the subway
tracks and colonies of rats,
        and possibly, improbably, Pound's poem—will last.

Arriving at Wallace Stevens in the 13th Week

I borrow an apple from Amy, place it on the carpet, and ask
what's changed, as we stare at this red and yellow
     freckled luminescence, our circled desks surrounding the mind
of nothing in our midst, altered by the various
     blues of our various guitars. We agree "Study of Two Pears"
is about pears, but "The Idea of Order at Key West"
     hums beyond the genius of these walls, and twenty pairs of eyes
puzzle over wide-open Nortons till Tony proclaims
     the singer in the poem to be the moon, since it's always pulling
at the tides, causing the ocean's roar. But
     tonight I stifle my irritation that he's found what isn't there
in the poem's portrayal of a woman's seaside
     singing. For once I let Tony be artificer of his own notes,
even if dimly starred, as he strides alongside
     the poem, thwarting my blessed rage for order honed by forty
years in classrooms. Yet I want him to slip
     barefoot into the poem's curling surf, want him to swim out
into the noctilucent swell of it with no guiding moon
     or pinpoint of harbor light, just the rise and fall of the waves
with their unpredictable lines, the undertow
     of the water's elastic weight, though I don't want him to drown,
and maybe I'm the one who's deaf to songs
     along the shore, to hymns that buzz beside my ears. Maybe
I can follow only one blackbird at a time,
     blind to the undulate spangles of another's sense of things.

Next-to-Last Week in the Senior Workshop

We're all chuckling over Brad's anti-football
                poem, and awed by Meg's poem
on puberty rites among the Diegueño
                of Baja, California, and, while everyone's
tuckered by this time in the semester, there's
                a warmth in the room that wasn't here
in September or even October when the temps
                hovered in the nineties, a comfort sewn
by fourteen minds bent over each other's
                poems so that week by week we've all
knitted into each other, and now,
                when it's time to end, it feels like layers
of skin being peeled. Sometimes, even
                the best students won't bother to find me
in my office after winter break to retrieve
                their portfolios. Most I'll never see
after finals. How I want to hang on, as if they're
                my own children, say, "Keep in touch,"
"Don't get lost." And though after each
                semester ends, it feels like sailing out
into open seas, unencumbered space,
                fresh winds, I always fear it may be
me I'm losing, as if, without those voices
                every week, I won't know what game
I'm playing, won't know what rituals
                to follow, as if I won't find land again.

Books, Bath Towels, and Beyond

After Gary asked, "Will we ever read
　　　　any normal people in this class?" and I quipped,
　　　　　　　"No, of course not," and after the laughter had quieted,
we ambled through "Song of Myself," celebrating
　　　　our "respiration and inspiration," traveling along
　　　　　　　with the voices of sailors, prostitutes, presidents, and tree-toads,
in sync with the poet's vision. No one
　　　　this time—not even Gary—grumbled about
　　　　　　　Whitman's disgusting ego, and yet when we came to the place
where God is "a loving bedfellow"
　　　　who leaves "baskets covered with white towels
　　　　　　　bulging the house with their plenty," I was the one who
wanted to stop. At that point, I've always
　　　　been puzzled. I get it that a lover could
　　　　　　　be like a god. But *towels*? We'd just finished *The House
of the Seven Gables*, and I wondered if
　　　　Hepzibah or Phoebe ever sold linens in their shop. Yet
　　　　　　　we never hear Hawthorne talking about blankets or sheets or
how anybody washes his face or her hands,
　　　　let alone armpits or "soft-tickling genitals"—leave
　　　　　　　those to Uncle Walt. The store Hepzibah opened: a first step
in easing the grip of her cursed
　　　　ancestors, of joining the sunlit world. Last summer
　　　　　　　when my husband and I moved back into our old house after
a massive redo, we gave away box after box
　　　　of sweaters and tchotchkes. We even disposed of old
　　　　　　　books, including those with my neon markings in the margins
blunt as Gary's outbursts in class: "Ugh,"
　　　　"NO," and "Wow!" It was time to loosen the mind
　　　　　　　beyond the nub of the old self. My mother used to huff through
the house every year like a great wind,
　　　　and when she settled down, not a doll over
　　　　　　　twelve months old remained, not a dress, not a scarf, not even

lint wisping in a drawer. One year during
           a flood, my husband's letters from lifelong friends
                      drowned in the garage, morphed back into pulp. I never hoped
the past would vanish into a blank, and yet,
           when Holgrave in the novel cries, "Shall we never,
                      never get rid of this Past?" I, too, want it washed clean, to wake
in the morning released from echoes
           of my father's muttered invectives, my mother's
                      searing tongue. I've now torn to rags the rust-stained towels
from my former marriage and
           my husband's bachelorhood sheets, raveled
                      threads drooping like fishnets. How Hawthorne's Phoebe
opened that heavy-lidded house
           to the light. I used to scorn her chirpy domesticity,
                      praying along with Emily Dickinson—whose balance
Gary had also questioned—"God keep me
           from what they call *households*." And yet, after
                      my husband and I returned to our remade, renewed house,
what did I do but go shopping
           for towels. Back and forth to seven strip malls,
                      bringing home only to return I don't know how many colors,
till finally, I settled on white. And as I
           pulled out my MasterCard to pay for the contents
                      of my brimming cart, a gaunt, wizened man entered
the check-out line, hands pressing
           to his chest two white towels just like mine,
                      eyes lifted to the ceiling as if in prayer. I doubt that Gary
would think it normal to greet the divine
           while clutching terry cloth. But now I see
                      that Whitman knew what fresh towels could mean for a dazed
and puffy face, white towels unspecked by blood
           or errant coils of hair, towels that spill from a basket
                      like sea-foam. Like cirrus clouds adrift while we're loafing
on tender, newly sprouted blades of grass
           growing from the loam under our boot soles,
                      from graves of the old and decaying, all we've finally buried.

In Our Class on Roethke

Jennifer's complaining he's really a wimp,
                    his endings don't grab her. "And what's more,
in 'The Waking,' he sounds drugged,
                    like maybe he's dying," says Jennifer, adding
          she feels the poem is about death, since
                    it made her depressed, especially "that worm
climbing the winding stair." I almost holler out
                    she's got it wrong, that's not the poem I've loved.
          But who can tell how light will take a tree,
                    predict the progressions of shadow shifting
into sun. We've just slipped back
                    into our chairs, after a trek across campus
          to watch Tibetan monks tip grains of sand
                    around edges of the mandala that tomorrow
they'll efface, an illustration of Wallace Stevens'
                    mantra we've discussed, the only constant is change.
          I'm grateful for Daniel, who says the poem
                    is about what the monks are doing, filling in
that space, grain of sand by grain of sand,
                    taking it slow. "And then, it'll all be gone," says Daniel,
          adding, "It's hard to imagine
                    investing so much in something that won't last."
A measured way, the monks' design.
                    And one I've tried to learn to practice, studying
          to forget the frantic hurry-skurry memorized
                    at my mother's knee. The last word she ever spoke
was "quick," and "quick" again, as if the dance
                    could never end too soon. Great Nature always
          has that other thing to do to us—but
                    now I guess I must explain how Roethke
suffered from despair, yet how he also
                    learned to sing and whistle, romping with the bears
          along the living ground. I say aloud,

"This poem is one I'd like someone to read
if there's a funeral when I die," and
                              Brittany says, "Oh please don't even think that way."
      These students here beside me, every
                  Thursday evening, all semester. A week
till finals, then it's over. Our syllables
                              commingling, little speech-threaders. They keep
      my shaking steady. Line by phrase,
                  word by breath, we learn by going, as we go.

Ending the Semester in American Lit

The guy who served as a lighthouse
    when discussions had grown so foggy I couldn't
        steer us back on course—the one who never missed
a class, who camped in my office every
    Wednesday afternoon obsessed with Bartleby
        and Ahab, made all A's and wrote a dynamite final—
hasn't turned in his long essay. Is he
    bleeding on a gurney in the ER, or moaning
        by the freeway in a pile of smashed glass and mangled
chrome? I email, and he shoots back, "I haven't
    written it." No apology, no excuse. I offer an
        extra day. No response, not even to say he prefers
not to. I want to harpoon that essay and
    splatter it onto my desk. I give him till
        midnight, remind him, bold font on the syllabus:
"No essay, no passing grade." Still silence,
    nada, no paper. Where *is* that essay? I feel
        like Herman's wife Lizzie, nagging him, or Carlyle,
insisting, "Produce! Produce!" Melville's
    narrator at least learned about his clerk's past
        at the dead letter office, but I have no idea where
this guy works, or if he does. Is he playing
    some kind of game, resisting like Bartleby,
        forcing me to play Ahab, hunt him down? Why
can't I just give him an F? I've become
    the narrator in Melville's story, his whole career
        questioned by the scrivener's refusals. Maybe I'm
remembering my years as a grad student
    when I skimped time with my son to write
        all those essays, the dread dissertation, and, then, later,
meet deadlines for grades, committee
    reports. Updating the CV to show every
        minuscule pebble I cast into the scholarly sea. All those

sleepy post-Christmas days I missed—leaving

    my boy and his dad in their jammies—to join

        the tangled academic throngs at the MLA. On this guy's

final exam he added a note that said

    our class had changed him, he'd been on course

        to become like Ahab, netting every A in sight, but after

finishing *Moby-Dick* and then reading

    Whitman, he decided to spend more time with

        his daughter, who's just learning to walk, and he didn't

want to miss a single one of her

    wobbling steps, he felt the pull to "loafe

        and invite" his soul. But I'm left here anchorless,

like Melville's ship the *Rachel*

    searching after her missing sailors, her lost children.

The Last Time I Taught Robert Frost

I shuddered when Olivia, who is writing her dissertation
      on dialectics of the self in Gloria Anzaldúa, announced she found him
lovely. "Lovely?" I cried, professional composure shot,
      my image of Frost collapsing suddenly as the Great Stone Face
on Cannon Mountain, the craggy Old Man fallen in shards
      to the ground. True, this was not on par with the vandalizing
of his house in Vermont, Homer Noble Farm's wicker chairs,
      wooden tables, dressers smashed and thrown into the fire to keep
the place warm while thirty kids swilled a hundred and fifty
      cans of Bud with a dozen bottles of Jack Daniel's, and threw up
on the floor. After all, Olivia wasn't saying she didn't like
      the poems, but *lovely?* A word my mother detested as phony,
like someone holding a pinkie straight out while drinking tea,
      the sort of word my grandmother used when vaguely praising
a Bartók piece, or a play she didn't understand. Like people
      saying, "How interesting," when what they really mean is, "Spare me
the details," or, "Could we change the subject." So when
      I asked Olivia what she meant by "lovely" and she talked about
the lush, long vowel sounds, I wondered why I'd felt stabbed,
      until I remembered my father's lying in the ICU, the fat respirator
tube jammed down his throat, the whoosh of forced breath
      fogging the glassed-in-room, and my stroking his forehead while
my father, whom I'd never seen cry, began to leak tears down
      his chiseled face. Finally, not knowing what more to do, I stood
by the window staring out at the New Hampshire pines
      and began reciting one of his favorite poems: "I must go down
to the seas again, to the lonely sea and the sky." He started
      to jerk, whole body spasms under the sheets, more tears carving
runnels down his cheeks, and I knew he wanted me to recite
      "Stopping By Woods," his most-loved poem and maybe mine too,
but I couldn't. I couldn't turn from that window looking
      out at the trees beyond the parking lot, the words to the one
poem I've known by heart for decades buried somewhere
      below my throat. He died the next day. Maybe that was why
I asked the class if we could recite it, if perhaps some of them

even had it memorized, and Denise and Lupe and Nathaniel actually
said they had. So we chanted it, the other eight of us

    reading from the Norton's crisp, white pages, but when we came
to the ending, not a single student needed to look down

    as we sang the last stanza all together. I can't explain it, but for once
something dark and deep entered among us in the overly

    air-conditioned room. As if we were all one self and yet still alone
in the cold, and wanting to stay. When we spoke again,

    we talked until I had to stand up, open the door, and tell them
to leave, say it was past time for their dinners and

    all the lovely, nagging promises waiting for them to keep.

Wendy Barker's novel in prose poems, *Nothing Between Us: The Berkeley Years* (runner-up for the Del Sol Prize) was released by Del Sol Press in 2009. Earlier full-length collections of poetry include *Poems from Paradise* (WordTech, 2005), *Way of Whiteness* (Wings Press, 2000), *Let the Ice Speak* (Ithaca House, 1991), and *Winter Chickens* (Corona Publishing, 1990). Wendy has also published four chapbooks, *From the Moon, Earth Is Blue* (Wings Press, 2015), *Things of the Weather* (Pudding House Press, 2009), *Between Frames* (Pecan Grove Press, 2006) and *Eve Remembers* (Aark Arts, 1996).

A selection of poems accompanied by autobiographical essays, *Poems' Progress* (Absey & Co.), appeared in 2002, and a collection of translations (with Saranindranath Tagore) from the Bengali of India's Nobel Prize-winning poet, *Rabindranath Tagore: Final Poems* (George Braziller, 2001), received the Sourette Diehl Fraser Award from the Texas Institute of Letters.

Wendy's poems and translations have appeared in many journals, including *Poetry, Southern Review, Georgia Review, Gettysburg Review, The American Scholar, Kenyon Review, New Letters, Nimrod, Stand, Partisan Review, Michigan Quarterly Review, Antioch,* and *Southern Poetry Review.* Her work has also been included in numerous anthologies, including *The Best American Poetry 2013* (eds. Denise Duhamel and David Lehman). Essays have appeared in such magazines as *Poets & Writers* and *Southwest Review.*

She has read her poetry at dozens of universities, bookstores, festivals, and conferences in the United States, Europe, and in India. As a scholar, she is the author of *Lunacy of Light: Emily Dickinson and the Experience of Metaphor* (Southern Illinois University Press, 1987) as well as co-editor (with Sandra M. Gilbert) of *The House Is Made of Poetry: The Art of Ruth Stone* (Southern Illinois University Press, 1996).

Recipient of an NEA fellowship, a Rockefeller residency fellowship at Bellagio, as well as other awards in poetry, including the Writers' League of Texas Book Award (which she has received twice, for *Way of Whiteness* in 2000 and for *Between Frames* in 2007) and the Mary Elinore Smith Poetry Prize from *The American Scholar,* she has also been a Fulbright senior lecturer in Bulgaria. Her work has been translated into Hindi, Chinese, Japanese, Russian, and Bulgarian.

She is poet-in-residence and the Pearl LeWinn professor of creative writing at the University of Texas at San Antonio, where she has taught since 1982. Wendy has one son, David Barker, and is married to the critic and biographer Steven G. Kellman.

Winners of the
John Ciardi Prize for Poetry:

The Resurrection Machine by Steve Gehrke, selected by Miller Williams

Kentucky Swami by Tim Skeen, selected by Michael Burns

Escape Artist by Terry Blackhawk, selected by Molly Peacock

Fence Line by Curtis Bauer, selected by Christopher Buckley

The Portable Famine by Rane Arroyo, selected by Robin Becker

Wayne's College of Beauty by David Swanger, selected by Colleen J. McElroy

Airs & Voices by Paula Bonnell, selected by Mark Jarman

Black Tupelo Country by Doug Ramspeck, selected by Leslie Adrienne Miller

Tongue of War by Tony Barnstone, selected by B. H. Fairchild

Mapmaking by Megan Harlan, selected by Sidney Wade

Secret Wounds by Richard M. Berlin, selected by Gary Young

Axis Mundi by Karen Holmberg, selected by Lorna Dee Cervantes

Beauty Mark by Suzanne Cleary, selected by Kevin Prufer

Border States by Jane Hoogestraat, selected by Luis J. Rodríguez

One Blackbird at a Time by Wendy Barker, selected by Alice Friman